j 503
D98f

DETROIT PUBLIC LIBRARY

P9-EFJ-230

DATE DUE

OCT '95

CH-R

First Math Dictionary

Richard W. Dyches
Jean M. Shaw
Elizabeth B.D. Heath

Illustrated by Czeslaw Sornat

Franklin Watts

New York • Chicago • London • Toronto • Sydney

The authors wish to thank the following people for their assistance in evaluating this manuscript.

James D. Cowles, Ph.D.
Department of Early Childhood Education
United States International University
San Diego, California

Helene Silverman, Ph.D.
Herbert H. Lehman College
City University of New York
Bronx, New York

Margaret Kasten, Ph.D.
Technology Consultant
Ohio Department of Education
Columbus, Ohio

Patricia M. Wilson, M.A.
Adjunct Professor of Education
Mercy College
Dobbs Ferry, New York

Marilyn S. Neil, Ph.D.
Associate Professor of Education
Georgia Southwestern College
Americus, Georgia

Editorial Development: The Pegasus Group
Design and Production: The Pegasus Group

For Katie and Matt
Jordana, Michael, and Kate

Library of Congress Cataloging-in-Publication Date
Dyches, Richard W.
First math dictionary / by Richard W. Dyches,
Jean M. Shaw, and Elizabeth B.D. Heath
p.   cm.
Summary: Illustrations and simple definitions introduce over
260 math terms.
ISBN 0-531-11111-3
1. Mathematics—Dictionaries, Juvenile.
[1. Mathematics—Dictionaries.]
I. Shaw, Jean M.   II. Title.
QA5.D93   1991
503–dc20
91-7527   CIP   AC

Copyright © 1991 by Franklin Watts, Inc.
All rights reserved
Printed in the United States of America
6   5   4   3   2

Dear Parent and Educator:

Math is an abstract and often difficult subject for children to comprehend in their early school years. However, in today's high-tech world it is especially important that children develop a strong foundation in the vocabulary of math so that they can increase their confidence as they learn harder concepts. This *First Math Dictionary,* designed for grades K-3, provides that foundation by defining more than 260 terms that must be mastered in order to effectively handle more complex math problems encountered in grades 4 and beyond.

Through the use of this reference book, math is demystified and becomes fun when it is learned by taking a trip with a special friend. Zebras, lions, tigers, and giraffes as well as other animals help explain such concepts as counting, addition, and measurement. Math is less abstract when the illustrations reinforce and explain the clearly written definitions. The learner *sees* the definitions, and a child's interest in math is enhanced when looking at visual representations such as the 5 bananas and 3 pineapples held by the smiling monkey that add up to 8 pieces of fruit.

We believe that this subject-focused dictionary and its companion, the *First Science Dictionary,* are unique in that they both teach a subject and encourage good reference skills by introducing the young reader to alphabetized key terms. The math dictionary also reflects an extensive review of the curriculum and follows the Standards of the National Council of Teachers of Mathematics. Futhermore, it correlates with all major math textbooks.

With the use of this important reference tool, we are confident that children will learn the math terminology they need both in their classrooms and in their everyday lives.

Sincerely,

Richard W. Dyches   Jean M. Shaw

ABOUT THE AUTHORS

Dr. Richard W. Dyches is a consultant and writer of educational materials for young children. A former elementary teacher and college professor, Dr. Dyches frequently lectures at national and international workshops and conferences. He lives in New York City.

Dr. Jean M. Shaw is a Professor of Elementary and Early Childhood Education at the University of Mississippi. She is a nationally known educator and author of many books for young children in the areas of math and science. Dr. Shaw lives in Oxford, Mississippi.

Elizabeth B.D. Heath has taught students in elementary schools for fourteen years, mostly the younger grades. She also has experience in the field of special education.

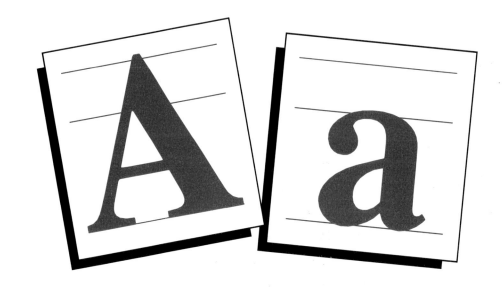

Aa

abacus

You use an **abacus** for counting. You count using the beads.

about

About means close to or almost. There are **about** 400 marbles in the box.

above

Above means over or higher. The kite is **above** the hippo.

addend

Addends are numbers that are added to get a sum.

addition

Addition is joining two or more addends or groups to find a sum.

after

After means later or following. 4 comes **after** 3.

alike

Things that are **alike** are the same in some way. The boxes are **alike**.

altogether

Altogether means how many in all. There are 8 oranges **altogether**.

amount

An **amount** can be measured. The **amount** on the scale is four pounds.

angle

When two rays meet, they form an **angle**.

approximate

You **approximate** by telling about how many or how much.
There are about 40 birds.

area

Area = 14 squares

Area is the number of square units needed to cover a region.

array

An **array** is an arrangement of numbers or objects with
the same number in each row.

Aa

When sets have the same number, one set has **as many as** the other.

An **attribute** is a special feature used to describe an object.

$$3 + 7 + 8 = 18$$
$$18 \div 3 = 6$$

An **average** tells what each number in a group would be if all the numbers were about the same. The **average** is also called the mean.

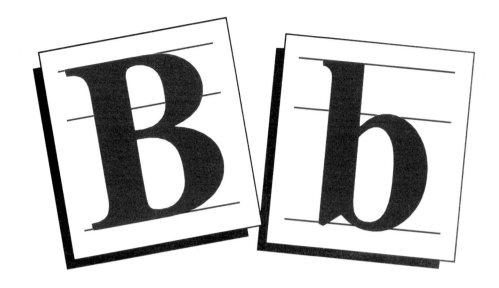

bar graph

A **bar graph** uses bars to show information.

base

base

A shape stands on its **base**.

basic facts

Operations with the numbers 0 to 9 are called **basic facts**.

before

Before means when something comes ahead of another. 7 comes **before** 8.

below

Below means under or lower. The lion is **below** the cat.

beside

Beside means next to another. The fox is sitting **beside** the cow.

between

When an object has something on either side of it, it is **between** them.

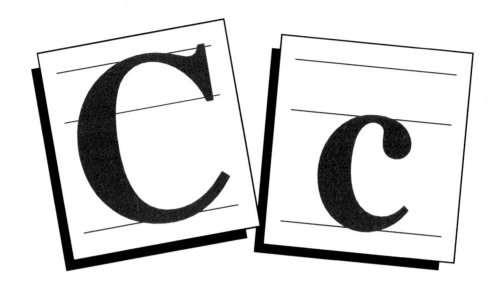

1, 2, 3, 4, and 1 more makes 5.

You **calculate** to find answers for number operations.

27 ÷ 9 = ?

A **calculator** can be used to add, subtract, multiply, divide, and do other operations.

calendar

A **calendar** is used to measure time and shows the order of days and months.

capacity

The **capacity** is the measure of how much something can hold.

cardinal numbers

The **cardinal numbers** are counting numbers that tell how many.

Cc

Celsius

Temperature in the metric system is measured in degrees **Celsius**.

cent

A penny is a coin worth one **cent**.
100 **cents** = 1 dollar

center

center

The **center** is a point in the middle of a shape.

centimeter

You use a **centimeter** to measure length.
100 **centimeters** = 1 meter

century

HAPPY 100th BIRTHDAY

A **century** is 100 years.

Cc

chance

Chance means something might happen. There is a **chance** of rain.

circle

A **circle** is a flat round shape. All points on the **circle** are the same distance from the center.

circle graph

A **circle graph** uses parts of a circle to show information about a whole.

classify

You **classify** by sorting into groups by an attribute.

clock

A **clock** is used to show time.

close/close to

If one thing is **close to** another, it is very near.

closed shape

A **closed shape** has no ends. It has no openings in it.

column

A **column** is a line of numbers or objects that goes up and down.

Cc

combination

A **combination** is a certain grouping of objects or numbers.

compare

You **compare** two amounts or sizes.

computer

A **computer** is a machine that helps people solve problems.

cone

A **cone** is a solid shape that comes to a point at one end. Its base is a circle.

congruent

Congruent shapes have the same size and shape. The squares are **congruent**.

corner

The **corner** is where sides meet.

count

...4, 5, 6, 7, 8, 9,...

You **count** by naming the numbers in order to tell how many.

cube

A **cube** is a solid shape. A **cube** has six square faces.

cubic unit

Cubic units are used to measure volume.

cup

You use a **cup** to measure capacity.
2 **cups** = 1 pint

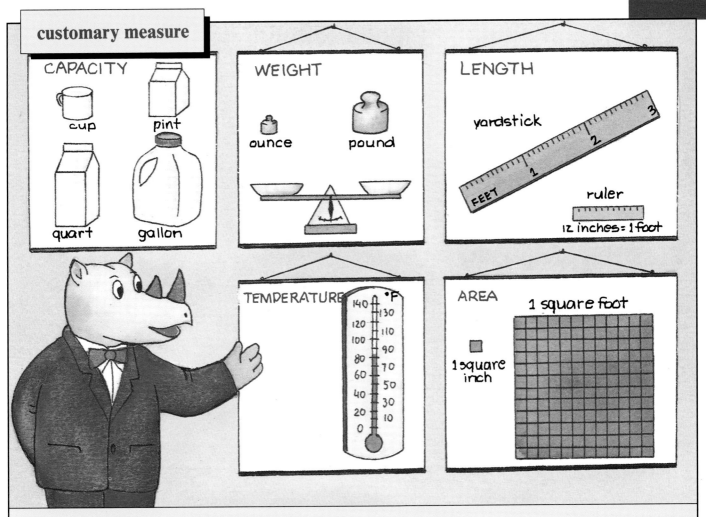

customary measure

Some **customary measures** are cup, pound, yard, and square inches.

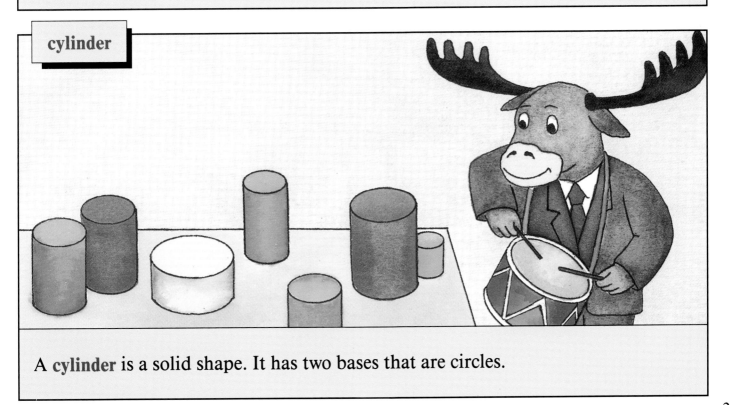

cylinder

A **cylinder** is a solid shape. It has two bases that are circles.

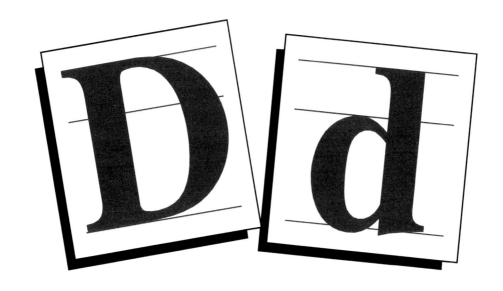

day

A **day** is used to measure time.
1 **day** = 24 hours

decimal

Our number system is a **decimal** system. It is based on ten and uses place value.

decimal point

You use a **decimal point** to write dollars and cents.

decimeter

You use a **decimeter** to measure length.
1 **decimeter** = 10 centimeters

degree

Temperature is measured in **degrees**.

denominator

In a fraction, the **denominator** tells the number of equal parts of the whole.

Dd

diagonal

diagonal

A **diagonal** is a line segment that joins opposite corners of a shape.

diameter

diameter

A **diameter** is a line segment that connects two points on a circle and passes through the center.

diamond

A **diamond** is a flat shape with four equal sides. A **diamond** is also called a rhombus.

difference

4 - 3 = 1

difference

The **difference** is the answer you get when subtracting.

different

Things that are not alike are **different**. The shapes are **different**.

digit

There are ten **digits** — 0, 1, 2, 3, 4, 5, 6, 7, 8, and 9. Numbers can have many **digits**.

digital clock

A **digital clock** shows time with numerals and has no hands.

dime

A **dime** is a coin worth ten cents.
1 **dime** = 10 pennies

Dd

division

$$9 \div 3 = 3$$

Division is separating groups into equal parts.

dollar

A **dollar** is paper money worth 100 cents.
1 **dollar** = 100 cents

double

You **double** when you find two times as much.

dozen

Twelve is another name for a **dozen**.

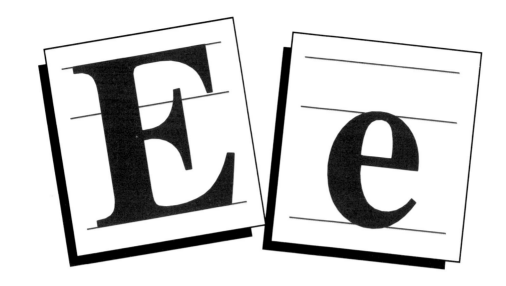

edge

An **edge** is the line segment where two faces of a solid shape meet.

equal

Amounts that are exactly the same are **equal**.

equally likely events

Equally likely events are those that have the same chance of happening.

equation

An **equation** is a number sentence. It shows that two amounts are equal.

equivalent

Equivalent amounts or groups are the same.

error

Ooops!

An **error** is a mistake. $2 + 2 \neq 5$
$2 + 2 = 4$

estimate

You **estimate** by guessing about how much or how many.

even

Two people can share an **even** number of things equally.

event

An **event** is something that could happen.

expanded form

356 = 300 + 50 + 6

Expanded form is a way to write numbers. It shows how much each digit is worth.

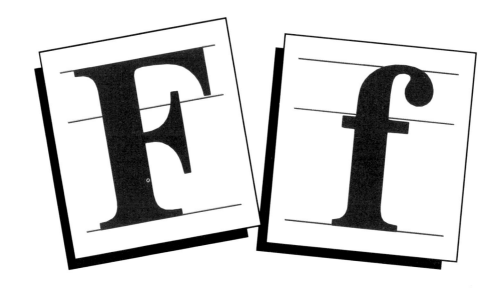

face

Any flat part of a solid shape is a **face**.

factor

$$4 \times 2 = 8$$
factors

Factors are numbers that are multiplied to get a product.

Fahrenheit

Temperature can be measured in degrees **Fahrenheit**. It is 30 degrees **Fahrenheit**

far

Far means distant.

fewer

Fewer is a smaller amount. The rhino has **fewer** crayons.

flip

You **flip** something by turning it over.

foot

You use a **foot** to measure length.
1 **foot** = 12 inches

fraction

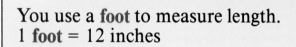

$\frac{3}{4}$ $\frac{2}{3}$

A **fraction** is part of a whole.

gallon

You use a **gallon** to measure capacity.
1 **gallon** = 4 quarts

geoboard

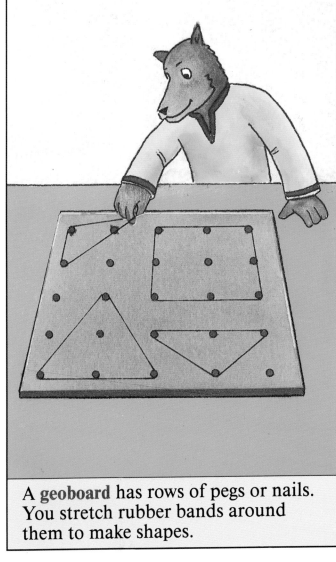

A **geoboard** has rows of pegs or nails.
You stretch rubber bands around
them to make shapes.

33

Gg

geometry

In **geometry,** you learn about flat shapes, solid shapes, lines, and angles.

gram

You use a **gram** to measure mass.
1 **gram** = 1,000 milligrams

graph

A **graph** is a drawing that shows information.

greater

Greater means more than or a larger amount. > means "is **greater** than."

greatest

greatest

The **greatest** means the largest in number or size.

group

A **group** is a set of things.

Gg

grouping property of addition

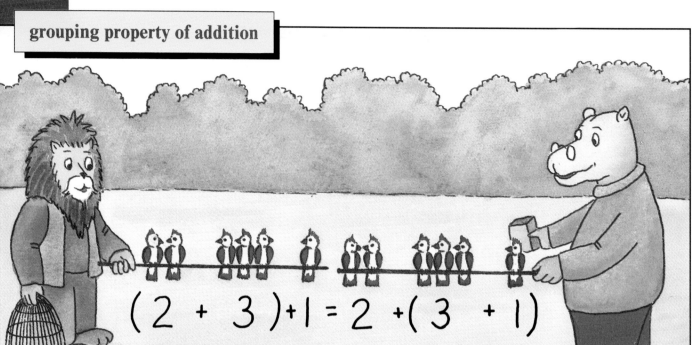

$$(2 + 3) + 1 = 2 + (3 + 1)$$

The **grouping property of addition** says that when you change the grouping of addends, you do not change the sum.

grouping property of multiplication

$$(2 \times 3) \times 4 = 2 \times (3 \times 4)$$
$$6 \times 4 = 2 \times 12$$
$$24 = 24$$

The **grouping property of multiplication** says that when you change the grouping of factors, you do not change the product.

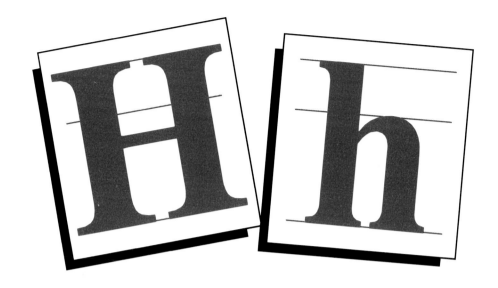

half

You get a **half** by dividing something into two equal parts.

half-dollar

A **half-dollar** is a coin worth 50 cents.
1 **half-dollar** = 50 cents

Hh

height

The **height** is the measure of something from top to bottom.

hexagon

A **hexagon** is a flat shape. A **hexagon** has six sides.

high

How high is the wall?

High means toward the sky or tall. The wall is five feet **high.**

horizontal

A line is **horizontal** if it goes across.

hour

An **hour** is used to measure time.
1 **hour** = 60 minutes

hundred

10 tens= 100

One **hundred** is a three-digit number.
1 **hundred** = 10 tens

hundreds chart

1	2	3	4	5	6	7	8	9	10
11	12	13	14	15	16	17	18	19	20
21	22	23	24	25	26	27	28	29	30
31	32	33	34	35	36	37	38	39	40
41	42	43	44	45	46	47	48	49	50
51	52	53	54	55	56	57	58	59	60
61	62	63	64	65	66	67	68	69	70
71	72	73	74	75	76	77	78	79	80
81	82	83	84	85	86	87	88	89	90
91	92	93	94	95	96	97	98	99	100

A **hundreds chart** is a chart with all
the numbers in order from 1 to 100.

hundreds place

hundreds	tens	ones
2	5	6

The digit in the **hundreds place** shows how many hundreds there are.

hundredth

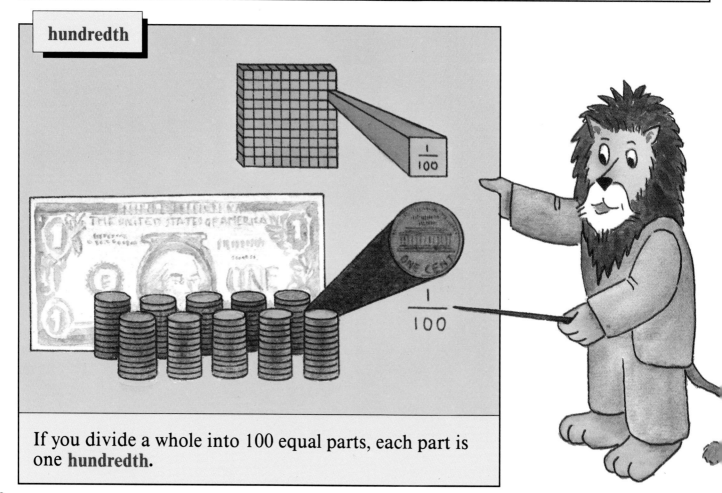

If you divide a whole into 100 equal parts, each part is one **hundredth**.

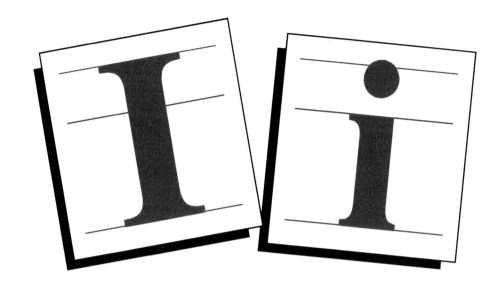

inch

You use an **inch** to measure length.
12 **inches** = 1 foot

inside

Inside is the opposite of outside. The monkey is **inside** the box.

intersection

intersection

An **intersection** is the place where lines or figures cross or meet.

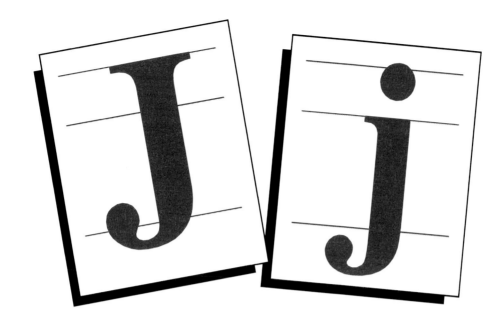

join

You **join** by putting things together.

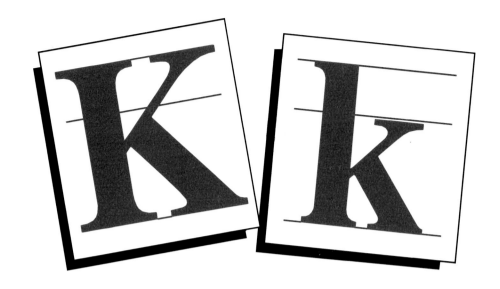

key

A **key** is a button you press on a calculator or computer.

kilogram

You use a **kilogram** to measure mass.
1 **kilogram** = 1,000 grams

kilometer

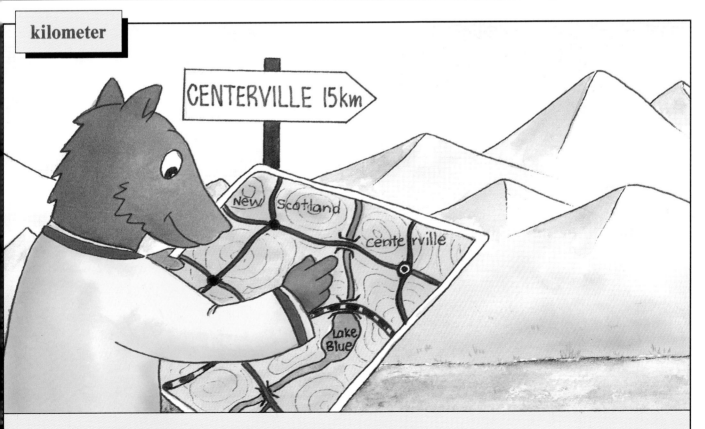

You use a **kilometer** to measure length or distance.
1 **kilometer** = 1,000 meters

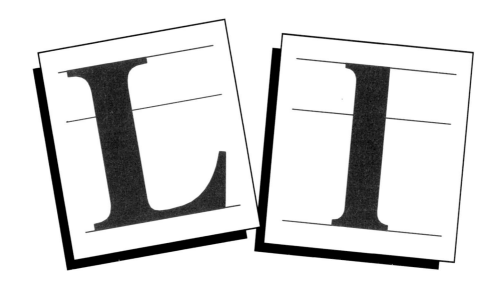

large   larger   largest

My foot is large.

My foot is larger than the fox's foot.

My foot is the largest of all.

Large means big.
Larger means the greater of two.
The **largest** is the greatest of three or more.

least

The **least** is the smallest number of three or more things.

left

LEFT TURN

Left means the opposite of right.

length

The **length** is the measure of something from end to end.

less

Less means fewer or a smaller amount. The lion has **less** money.

likely event

A **likely event** is something that will probably happen. It is likely to snow.

line

A **line** goes on in two opposite directions without end.

line graph

Children who bring an apple as a snack.

A **line graph** uses points and lines to show information.

line segment

A **line segment** is a part of a line.

liter

You use a **liter** to measure capacity.
1 **liter** = 1,000 milliliters

logic

Logic is a reasonable way to study and solve a problem.

long

Long tells you about length or time.
Long also is the opposite of short.

low

Low means close to the ground.

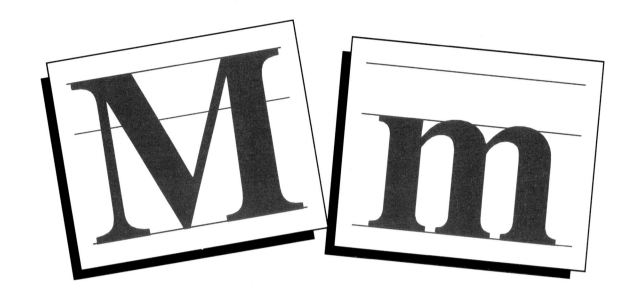

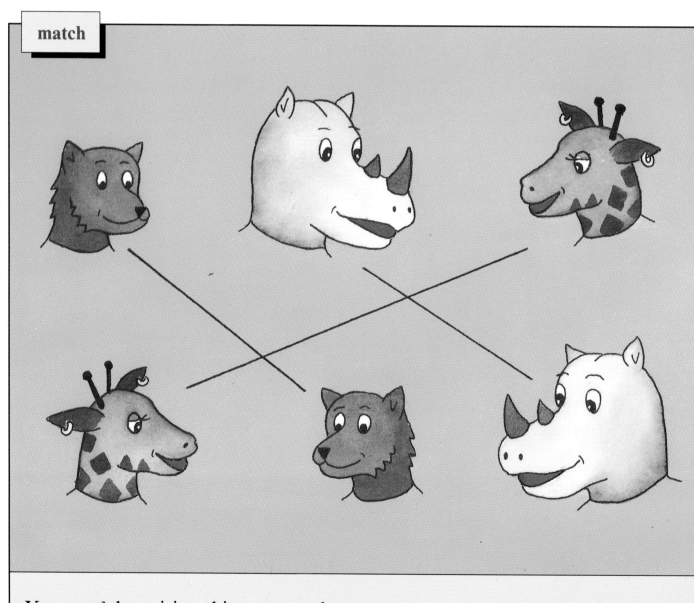

match

You **match** by pairing objects or numbers.

measure

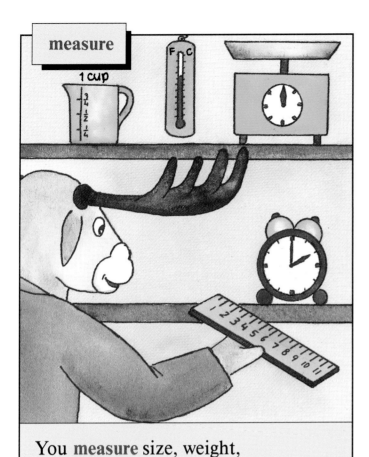

You **measure** size, weight, temperature, capacity, and time.

measuring cup

You use a **measuring cup** to measure capacity.

mental math

You use **mental math** to solve problems in your head.

meter

You use a **meter** to measure length.
1 **meter** = 100 centimeters

metric measure

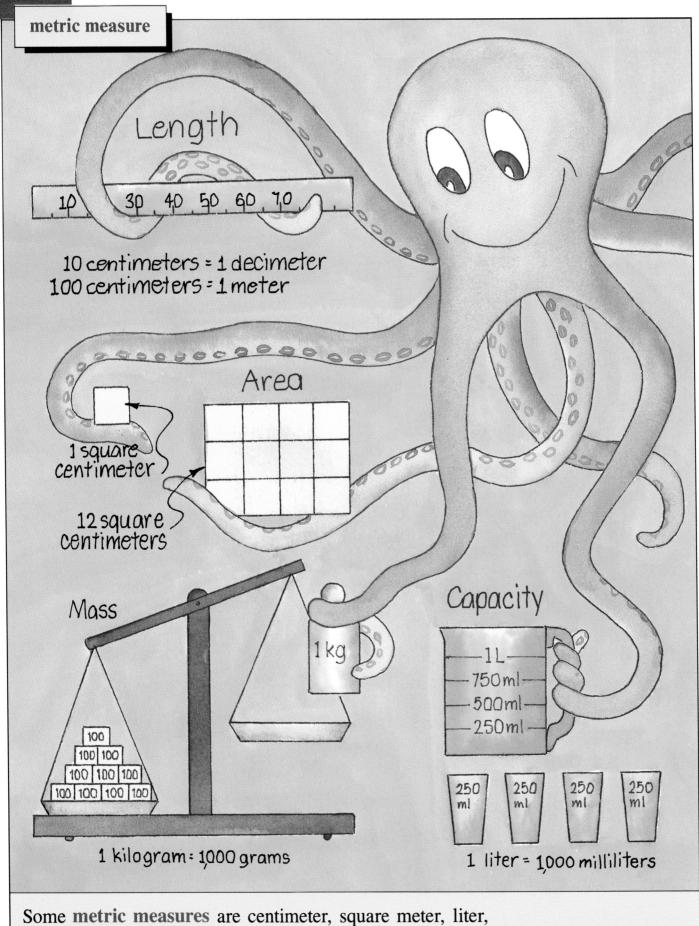

Length

10 centimeters = 1 decimeter
100 centimeters = 1 meter

Area

1 square centimeter

12 square centimeters

Mass

1 kg

1 kilogram = 1,000 grams

Capacity

1L
750 ml
500 ml
250 ml

250 ml   250 ml   250 ml   250 ml

1 liter = 1,000 milliliters

Some **metric measures** are centimeter, square meter, liter, and kilogram.

mile

HOME 5 MILES

You use a **mile** to measure length or distance.
1 **mile** = 5,280 feet

milliliter

You use a **milliliter** to measure capacity.
1,000 **milliliters** = 1 liter

minus

5 ☐ 1 = 4

minus sign

Minus is a sign for subtraction.

minute

In one minute, I can
• bounce a ball 30 times
• skip rope 50 times

A **minute** is used to measure time.
60 **minutes** = 1 hour

mirror image

A **mirror image** is a reflection that is exactly the same as the original.

missing addend

3 + ☐ = 5

missing addend

A **missing addend** is a number needed to complete the sum in a number sentence.

mixed number

$3\frac{1}{2}$

A **mixed number** has a whole number part and a fraction part.

model

$2 \times 5 = \square$

A **model** is something you make, write, or draw. It can help you solve a problem.

money

You use **money** to buy things or to save. **Money** comes in coins and paper.

month

A **month** is used to measure time.
12 **months** = 1 year

Mm

more

More means a greater amount. The cat has **more** snowballs.

multiple

$(2 \times 3 = 6)$ 6 is a multiple of 3
$(3 \times 3 = 9)$ 9 is a multiple of 3
$(4 \times 3 = 12)$ 12 is a multiple of 3
$(5 \times 3 = 15)$ 15 is a multiple of 3
$(6 \times 3 = 18)$ 18 is a multiple of 3
$(10 \times 3 = 30)$ 30 is a multiple of 3

Multiples are products that have one factor that is the same.

multiplication

$$4 \times 3 = \square$$

$$3 \quad + \quad 3 \quad + \quad 3 \quad + \quad 3$$

Multiplication is a short way to find a sum when the addends are the same.

Near means the same as close to.
Nearer is the closer of two.
The **nearest** is closest of three or more.

Nn

nickel

A **nickel** is a coin worth five cents.
1 **nickel** = 5 pennies

number

...9, 10, 11, 12, 13...

You can use **numbers** to count. A **number** tells you how many.

number line

A **number line** is a model that shows numbers in order.

$$7 - 3 = 4$$

A **number sentence** shows how numbers and operations are related.

A **numeral** is the written form of a number. 5 and 3 are **numerals.**

$$\frac{4}{5} \leftarrow \text{numerator}$$

In a fraction, the **numerator** tells how many parts you have.

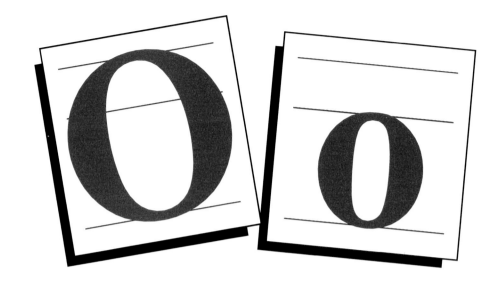

objective

An **objective** is a goal. The **objective** is to build a bookcase.

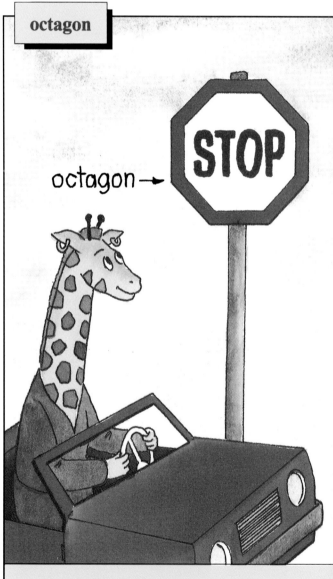

octagon

octagon →

An **octagon** is a flat shape. An **octagon** has eight sides.

odd

Two people cannot share an **odd** number of things equally.

one

One means a single thing.

ones place

hundreds	tens	ones
9	3	6

The digit in the **ones place** shows how many ones there are.

one-to-one

Two groups can be matched **one-to-one** An object in one group is matched to an object in the other group.

Oo

open shape

An **open shape** has two ends that do not meet.

operation

Some of the math **operations** are addition, subtraction, multiplication, and division.

opposite

Opposite means in a different direction. Down is the **opposite** of up.

order

To put things in **order** means to arrange them in a logical way.

order property of addition

$$2+1 = 1+2$$

The **order property of addition** says that when you change the order of the addends, you do not change the sum.

order property of multiplication

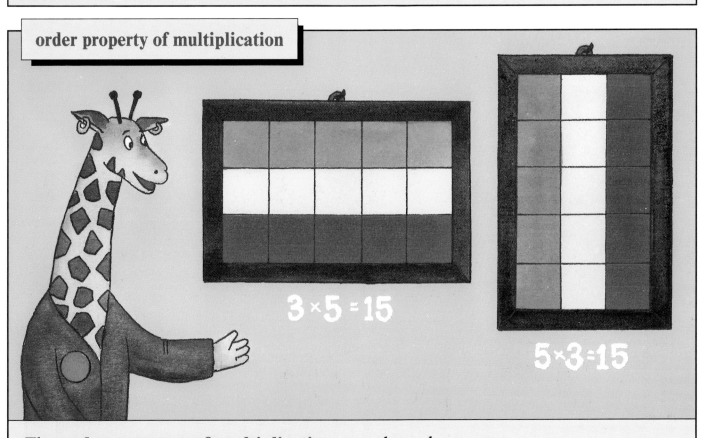

$$3 \times 5 = 15$$

$$5 \times 3 = 15$$

The **order property of multiplication** says that when you change the order of the factors, you do not change the product.

ordinal

You use an **ordinal** number to show position.
The red car is first.

ounce

You use an **ounce** to measure weight or capacity. 16 **ounces** = 1 pound
16 fluid **ounces** = 1 pint

outside

Outside is the opposite of inside.
Three books are **outside** the box.

oval

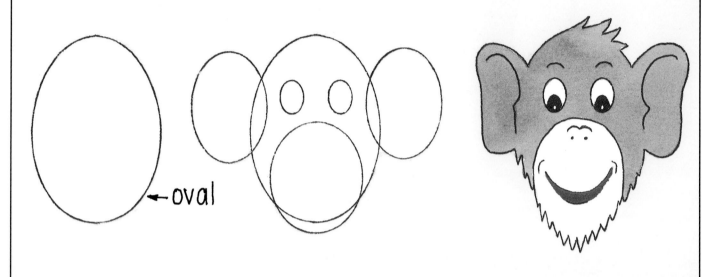

←oval

An **oval** is a flat shape.

over

Over means above or higher. The cars go **over** the trucks.

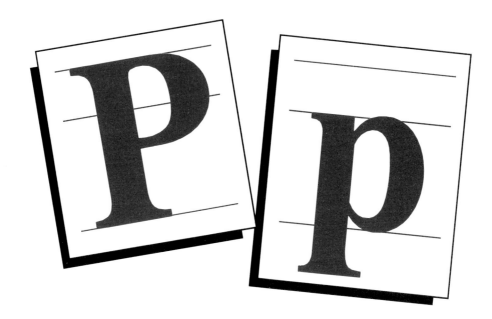

pair

A **pair** is a group of two.

parallel

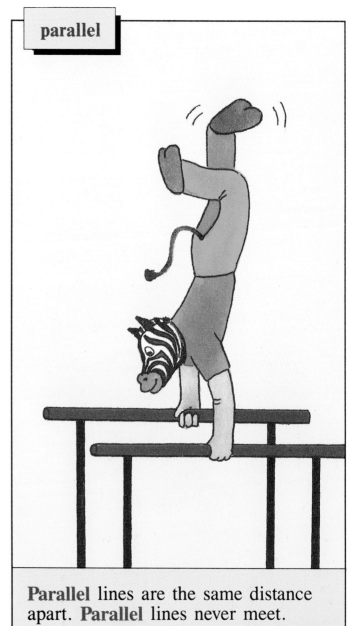

Parallel lines are the same distance apart. **Parallel** lines never meet.

parallelogram

A **parallelogram** is a flat shape with four sides. The opposite sides are parallel.

part

A **part** is a piece of an object, a group, or an amount.

pattern

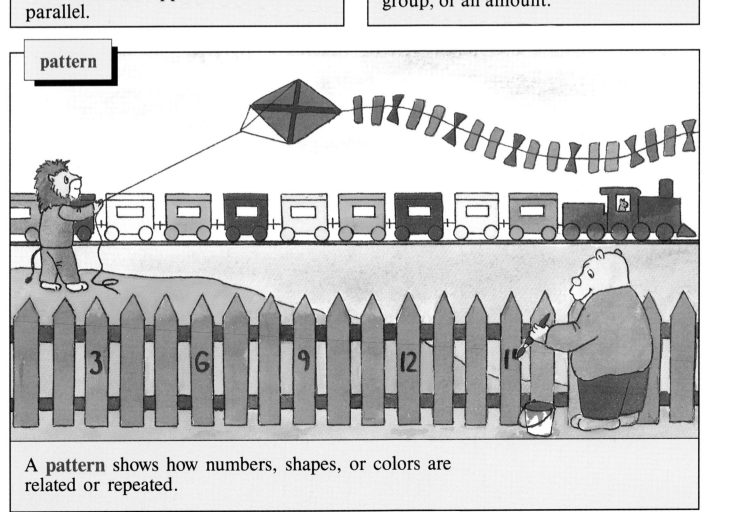

A **pattern** shows how numbers, shapes, or colors are related or repeated.

Pp

pattern blocks

Pattern blocks are shapes of different sizes and colors.

penny

A **penny** is a coin worth one cent.

pentagon

← pentagon

A **pentagon** is a flat shape. A **pentagon** has five sides.

percent

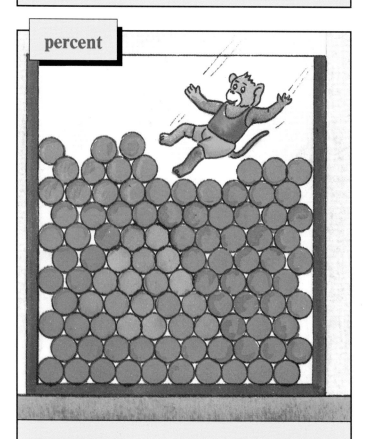

Percent means a part of 100. 20 **percent** of the balls are blue.

perimeter

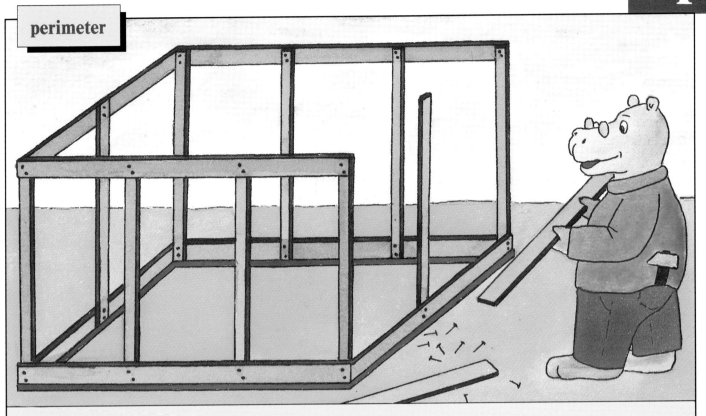

The **perimeter** is the distance around a flat shape.

pictograph

A **pictograph** uses pictures to show information. It is also called a picture graph.

pint

You use a **pint** to measure capacity.
1 **pint** = 2 cups

Pp

place value

Hundreds	Tens	Ones	Hundreds	Tens	Ones	Hundreds	Tens	Ones
1	4	2	4	2	1	2	1	4

In **place value** the position of a number shows how much
it is worth.

70

plane

A **plane** is a flat surface. A **plane** goes on forever in all directions.

plane shape

A **plane shape** is flat. You can draw a **plane shape** but you cannot pick it up.

plus

$3+1=4$

plus sign

Plus is a sign for addition.

point

A **point** is one place on a line or on a flat surface.

polygon

A **polygon** is a flat shape. A **polygon** has three or more sides.

pound

You use a **pound** to measure weight.
1 **pound** = 16 ounces

prism

A **prism** is a solid shape. The faces have four sides. The bases are polygons.

probability

Probability is the chance that something will happen.

Pp

problem

A **problem** is something that needs an answer.

problem solving

Problem solving is looking for an answer.

product

The **product** is the answer you get when multiplying.

quart

You use a **quart** to measure capacity.
4 **quarts** = 1 gallon

quarter

A **quarter** is a coin worth 25 cents.
1 **quarter** = 25 pennies

quotient

$9 \div 3 = 3$
quotient

The **quotient** is the answer you get when dividing.

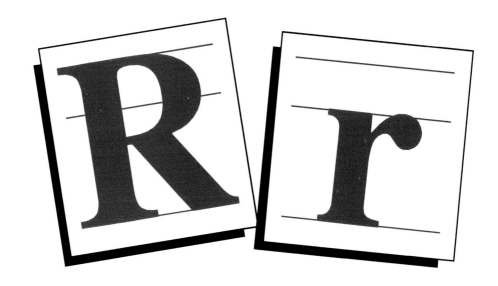

A **radius** is a line segment from the center of a circle to a point on the circle.

A **ratio** compares two amounts.

ray

A **ray** starts at a point and goes on in one direction without end.

rectangle

A **rectangle** is a flat shape. It has four right angles and two pairs of equal sides.

rectangular prism

A **rectangular prism** is a solid shape with six faces. The faces are rectangles.

region

A **region** is part of a flat shape.

regroup

You can **regroup** when you add or subtract. You can trade 10 ones for 1 ten or 1 hundred for 10 tens.

remainder

$13 \div 3 = 4 \text{ R}1$

The **remainder** is what is left over when you divide.

rename

$\frac{1}{2}$

$\frac{1}{2}$ $\frac{2}{4}$

$\frac{4}{8}$

5

$2 + 3$

$1 + 4$

You **rename** a number by giving it another name.

rhombus

A **rhombus** is a flat shape. A **rhombus** has four equal sides.

right

Right is the opposite of left.

right angle

A **right angle** is a square corner. It is shaped like the corner of a piece of paper.

Roman numerals

Roman numerals are symbols used to write numbers. The values of the symbols are added or subtracted.

round

A **round** shape has no straight lines and no corners.

row

A **row** is a line of numbers or objects that goes across.

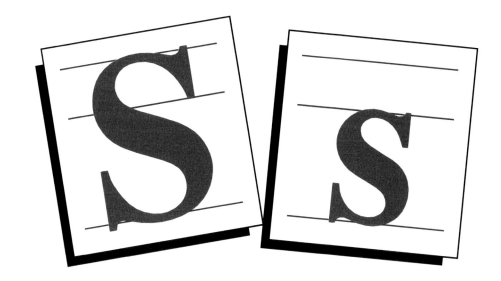

same

When things are the **same**, they are alike.

sample

A **sample** is a small group chosen by chance. It tells about a larger group.

Ss

A **scale** is used to measure weight.

A **second** is used to measure time.
60 **seconds** = 1 minute

A **set** is a group of things.

shape

Everything you see, draw, or pick up has a **shape**.

Ss

short
← pants

Short tells you about length or time.
Short is the opposite of long.

side

side

Sides are the line segments that form a shape.

sign

$$5 + 5 = 10$$

$$7 - 2 \neq 4$$

$$4 \times 3 = 12$$

$$15 \div 3 = 5$$

$$6 > 1$$

$$7 < 9$$

A math **sign** gives important information in a number sentence.

similar

When objects have the same shape, they are **similar**. The triangles are **similar**.

size

The **size** tells you how large or small an object is.

skip-count

You **skip-count** by counting groups of the same size.

Ss

Small means not great in size.
Smaller is the lesser of two.
The **smallest** is the least of three or more.

solid shape

A **solid shape** has the three dimensions — length, width, and height.

solve

You **solve** a problem by finding an answer.

sort

You **sort** by separating related things into groups.

sphere

A **sphere** is a solid shape with no faces or edges. A ball is a **sphere**.

square

A **square** is a flat shape. It has four equal sides and four right angles.

square units

Square units are used to measure area.

standard form

In **standard form**, digits and place value are used to write numbers.

subtraction

Subtraction is finding the difference between two numbers.

sum

$$5 + 3 = 8$$

sum

The **sum** is the answer you get when adding.

symbol

You use a **symbol** in place of words.

symmetry

line of symmetry

Two parts of a shape that match exactly have **symmetry**.

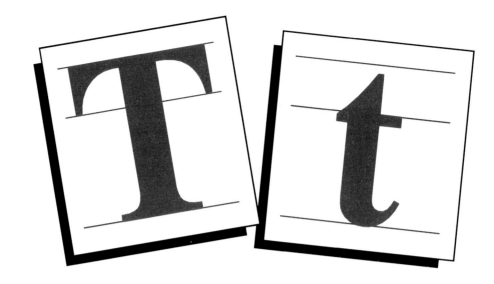

table

A **table** is a list with rows and columns. It helps you put information in order.

tablespoon

You use a **tablespoon** to measure capacity.
1 **tablespoon** = 3 teaspoons

tally

A **tally** is a series of marks made to keep a count.

teaspoon

3 teaspoons = 1 tablespoon

You use a **teaspoon** to measure capacity.
3 **teaspoons** = 1 tablespoon

temperature

Temperature is the measure of how hot or cold something is.

Tt

ten

Ten is the smallest two-digit number. You can group things by **ten**.

1 **ten** = 10 ones

tens place

The blue digit in the **tens place** shows how many tens there are.

thermometer

A **thermometer** is used to measure temperature. It is marked in degrees.

thousand

A **thousand** is a four-digit number.

1 **thousand** = 10 hundreds

three-digit

298

hundreds	tens	ones
2	9	8

A **three-digit** number is one that has hundreds, tens, and ones places.

three-dimensional

height
width
length

A **three-dimensional** shape is a solid shape with length, width, and height.

time

Time tells how long something takes. A clock and a calendar show **time**.

ton

1 ton

You use a **ton** to measure weight or mass. 1 **ton** = 2,000 pounds
1 metric **ton** = 1,000 kilograms

total

The **total** is the whole amount. There are a **total** of 11 animals.

triangle

A **triangle** is a flat shape. A **triangle** has three sides.

turn

You **turn** by changing directions.

two-digit

A **two-digit** number is one that has a tens place and a ones place.

two-dimensional

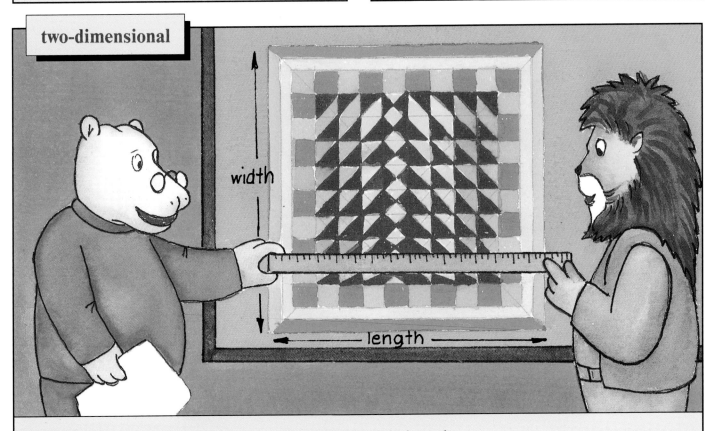

A **two-dimensional** shape is a flat shape with length and width.

under

Under means below or lower. The kitten is **under** the table.

unequal

Amounts are **unequal** if they are not the same.
≠ means "is not equal to."

unlikely event

An **unlikely event** is something that probably will
not happen.

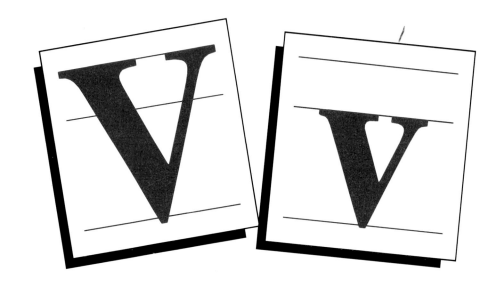

vertex

A **vertex** is a corner of a plane shape or a solid shape.

vertical

A line is **vertical** if it goes straight up and down.

volume

The **volume** is the number of cubic units needed to fill a solid shape.

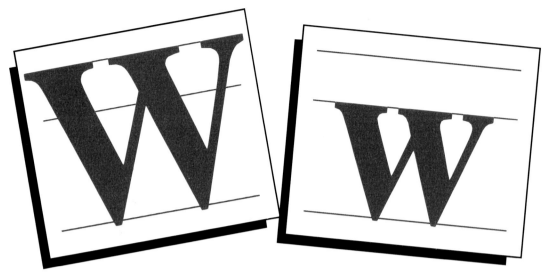

week

A **week** is used to measure time.
1 **week** = 7 days

weight

Weight is the measure of how heavy something is.

whole

whole

The **whole** is the entire amount or shape.

whole numbers

0 1 2
3 4
5

Whole numbers are zero and the counting numbers.

width

width

The **width** is the measure of something from side to side.

yard

You use a **yard** to measure length.
1 **yard** = 3 feet
1 **yard** = 36 inches

year

A **year** is used to measure time.
1 **year** = 12 months

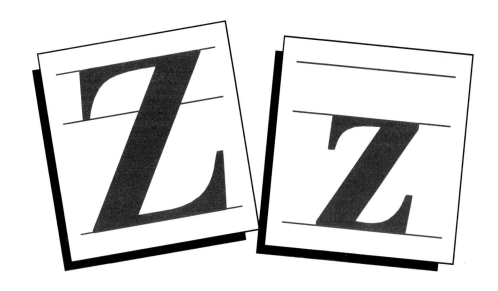

zero

Zero means there are no objects in the group.

zero property of addition

$$4 + 0 = 4$$

The **zero property of addition** says that if you add zero to any number, the sum is that number.

zero property of multiplication

$$6 \times 0 = 0$$

The **zero property of multiplication** says that if you multiply any number by zero, the product is always zero.